20 A couple celebrating their marriage

28 Remembering those we loved

How to use this book

People who follow the Islam religion are known as **Muslims**. This book tells you what it is like to be Muslim and about the special times, customs and beliefs of Muslims.

Finding your way

The pages in this book have been carefully planned to make it easy for you to find out about Islam. Here are two examples with explanations about the different features. Look at the Contents pages too, to read about each section.

Bold words in the text are explained more fully in the glossary on page 30.

Celebrating the birth of a baby

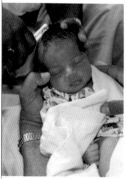

Seven days after a baby is born, Muslims have a celebration called Aqiqah. They use special customs to thank God for the gift of a baby and to share their happiness with other people.

At the Aqiqah

Goat or lamb meat is shared with friends and family or given to the poor. The baby's hair is shaved and weighed. In the past, parents gave an equal weight of silver to people in need. Now they usually give money.

Parents announce their baby's name at the Aqiqah. They choose from a book of Muslim names. Sometimes boys are named after prophets (important teachers in the past). Ibrahim (Abraham), Isa (Jesus), Musa (Moses) and Muhammad are popular names.

This baby girl is having her hair shaved by her uncle.

Hiba is 9 years old. She lives in the UK. She describes her baby sister's Aqiqah party.

My baby sister was born in the summer holidays. We had an Aqiqah in the garden with the best barbecue I've ever had. So many people came. They brought presents for my sister. We named her Maryam, which is the name of a chapter in the **Qur'an** (the Islamic holy book) that tells the story of Mary, the mother of Jesus. We believe Jesus was a Prophet of God and his mother was a special lady.

Case studies give a Muslim person's own experience of a custom described in the section.

This Arabic writing is made up of the words *Salla-llahu alaihi wa sallam*, which means "peace and blessings of **Allah** upon him". The words are used by Muslims every time the Prophet Muhammad is mentioned. Similar respect is given to other prophets.

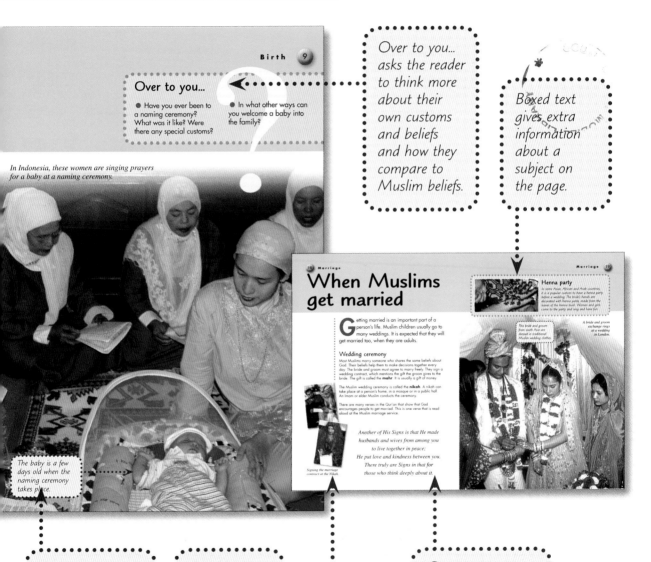

Over to you... asks the reader to think more about their own customs and beliefs and how they compare to Muslim beliefs.

Boxed text gives extra information about a subject on the page.

Comments give additional information about something specific in a picture.

Captions give a short description of a picture.

Quotes come from different Muslim teachings, and are translated from Arabic.

Over to you...

● Have you ever been to a naming ceremony? What was it like? Were there any special customs?

● In what other ways can you welcome a baby into the family?

In Indonesia, these women are singing prayers for a baby at a naming ceremony.

The baby is a few days old when the naming ceremony takes place.

When Muslims get married

Getting married is an important part of a person's life. Muslim children usually go to many weddings. It is expected that they will get married too, when they are adults.

Wedding ceremony

Most Muslims marry someone who shares the same beliefs about God. Their beliefs help them to make decisions together every day. The bride and groom must agree to marry freely. They sign a wedding contract, which mentions the gift the groom gives to the bride. The gift is called the **mahr**. It is usually a gift of money.

The Muslim wedding ceremony is called the **nikah**. A nikah can take place at a person's home, in a mosque or in a public hall. An Imam or elder Muslim conducts the ceremony.

There are many verses in the Qur'an that show that God encourages people to get married. This is one verse that is read aloud at the Muslim marriage service.

Another of His Signs is that He made husbands and wives from among you to live together in peace; He put love and kindness between you. There truly are Signs in that for those who think deeply about it.

Signing the marriage contract at the nikah.

Henna party

In some Asian, African and Arab countries, it is a popular custom to have a henna party before a wedding. The bride's hands are decorated with henna paste, made from the leaves of the henna bush. Women and girls come to the party and sing and have fun.

This bride and groom from south Asia are dressed in traditional Muslim wedding clothes.

A bride and groom exchange rings at a wedding in London.

A new baby is born

It's an amazing time when a baby is born. There are so many questions. Is it a boy or a girl? Has she got blue eyes or brown? People around the world celebrate a baby's birth in different ways.

Remembering God

A Muslim family welcomes a new baby by remembering God (Allah) and hoping the child will grow up to follow God's teachings. The first thing the baby hears is the Call to Prayer, the **Adhan**. The Adhan is a verse in **Arabic** that calls Muslims to prayer. It expresses a Muslim's important belief in one God and **Muhammad** ﷺ as the messenger of God.

A father whispers the Adhan in his baby's right ear.

The mu'adhin raises his hands to his ears to show he is going to give the Adhan.

The Adhan

This is some of the Adhan in English: "God is most great. I bear witness that none must be worshipped but God. I bear witness that Muhammad is the messenger of God. Come to prayer." In Muslim countries, every **mosque** *has a* **mu'adhin**, *who gives the Adhan five times a day to call the people to prayer. His call is heard across villages and towns.*

Family traditions

In some families, a parent or grandparent crushes a sweet fruit called a date and rubs the juice on the baby's gums. Some people use a drop of honey. This custom started when the **Prophet** Muhammad rubbed date juice on a baby's gums.

Family and friends say this prayer to congratulate the parents. It reminds them that a baby is a blessing from God and wishes the baby a long, healthy and good life.

The sweetness of dates and honey encourages the baby to start sucking and drinking milk.

May God bless you with His gift to you,
And may you give thanks.
May the child have a long life,
And may you be granted her goodness.

Celebrating the birth of a baby

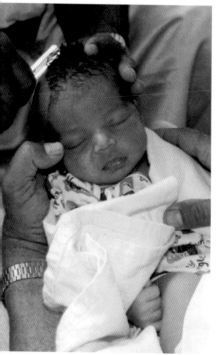

This baby girl is having her hair shaved by her uncle.

Seven days after a baby is born, Muslims have a celebration called an **Aqiqah**. They use special customs to thank God for the gift of a baby and to share their happiness with other people.

At the Aqiqah

Goat or lamb meat is shared with friends and family or given to the poor. The baby's hair is shaved and weighed. In the past, parents gave an equal weight of silver to people in need. Now they usually give money.

Parents announce their baby's name at the Aqiqah. They choose from a book of Muslim names. Sometimes boys are named after prophets (important teachers in the past). Ibrahim (Abraham), Isa (Jesus), Musa (Moses) and Muhammad are popular names.

Hiba is 9 years old. She lives in the UK. She describes her baby sister's Aqiqah party.

My baby sister was born in the summer holidays. We had an Aqiqah in the garden with the best barbecue I've ever had. So many people came. They brought presents for my sister. We named her Maryam, which is the name of a chapter in the **Qur'an** (the Islamic holy book) that tells the story of Mary, the mother of Jesus. We believe Jesus was a Prophet of God and his mother was a special lady.

A journey through life in
Islam

Suma Din

Contents

Published by A & C Black
Publishers Limited
36 Soho Square
London W1D 3QY
www.acblack.com

ISBN 978-1-4081-2966-1

Copyright © A & C Black Publishers
Limited 2010

Series concept: Suma Din
Series consultant: Lynne Broadbent
Created by Bookwork Ltd, Stroud, UK

A CIP catalogue record for this book is
available from the British Library.

A & C Black uses paper produced with
elemental chlorine-free pulp, harvested
from managed sustainable forests. It
is natural, renewable and recyclable.
The logging and manufacturing process
conform to the environmental regulations
of the country of origin.

Printed in China by Leo Paper Products

All the internet addresses given in this
book were correct at the time of going to
press. The author and publishers regret
any inconvenience caused if addresses
have changed or sites have ceased to
exist, but can accept no responsibility for
any such changes.

Over to you...

● Have you ever been to a naming ceremony? What was it like? Were there any special customs?

● In what other ways can you welcome a baby into the family?

In Indonesia, these women are singing prayers for a baby at a naming ceremony.

The baby is a few days old when the naming ceremony takes place.

Sharing a special time

Some Muslim families don't hold an Aqiqah party. Instead, they send money to people who don't have enough food, shelter or medicine. They give money to an **aid** organisation like Muslim Hands, which will give the money to people who need it.

Caring for other people

The Qur'an teaches Muslims that they should care for **orphans**. The organisation Muslim Hands runs schools and orphanages for children around the world. When families give money to Muslim Hands instead of having an Aqiqah party, they are sharing their celebration with children who are not lucky enough to have a family.

Ismail Abdullah works in Sudan in Africa for Muslim Hands. He explains how he used the money given by a family in the UK.

Sana and Hamza Ali had a baby girl called Aisha in the UK. They gave £45 to Muslim Hands. We used the money in Sudan to buy food. Volunteers at the School of Excellence in the city of Omdurman helped to clean and cook the meat. In the afternoon, the school children enjoyed a special meal of rice, vegetables and goat meat. I sent photographs of the Aqiqah back to our office in the UK so that Sana and Hamza could see the celebration.

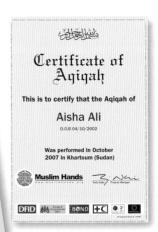

بسم الله الرحمن الرحيم

Certificate of Aqiqah

This is to certify that the Aqiqah of

Aisha Ali

D.O.B 04/10/2002

Was performed in October 2007 in Khartoum (Sudan)

Muslim Hands

Muslim Hands made a certificate for Aisha to show they had held an Aqiqah for her.

> *The most excellent charity is that you feed a hungry person.*

Orphans at the Omdurman School of Excellence in Sudan enjoyed the Aqiqah meal.

Why do people give money?

Giving someone money, food, help or time are all forms of **charity**. Prophet Muhammad ﷺ encouraged people to be charitable every day by doing simple things like this:

- Removing something harmful from a pathway
- Comforting somebody who is sad
- Caring for a hungry animal
- Planting seeds or trees
- Visiting someone who is ill
- Giving a homeless person shelter
- Providing food for a hungry person

Growing up as a Muslim child

Muslim teachings say that all children must be cared for with kindness and respect. Prophet Muhammad ﷺ said, "Be kind and noble to our children and make their habits and manners good and beautiful."

Learning from faith

When Muslim children learn about their faith, they learn how to behave the right way. They learn good manners and what is right and wrong. For example, they learn that it is wrong to hurt someone with words or actions.

Praying

Young Muslim children learn about their faith from their parents and by going to the mosque. They may pray with their parents before breakfast. Hearing the Qur'an at the start of the day will help them to feel peaceful.

These young girls are learning how to pray at Woking Mosque in England.

Over to you...

● What do you think are the three most important things all children need?

● Why is it important to have a good education?

● Who teaches you what is the right way to behave?

Many Muslim women cover their head as part of their Muslim culture.

Lots to learn

The Qur'an is written in Arabic so Muslim children learn to read Arabic when they are as young as six years old. They also learn what the Qur'an means by reading the meaning in English. At school, at home or in the mosque – all learning is important. That is why Prophet Muhammad said,

A father gives a child nothing better than a good education.

A Muslim mother helps her children learn what the words of the Qur'an mean.

Starting to pray five times a day

As Muslim children grow up, it becomes important for them to practise their faith every day. They learn how to perform the five daily prayers called **Salah**. These prayers are said in Arabic, in the way that was taught by the Prophet Muhammad ﷺ.

Prayer and Makkah

When Muslims pray, they face towards **Makkah**, a holy city in Saudi Arabia where the Prophet Abraham built a place of worship. The Sacred Mosque, the most holy place for Muslims, is in Makkah.

The prayer halls in a mosque are decorated with verses from the Qur'an and beautiful patterns. There are no pictures because Muslims do not worship images or statues.

Wudu

Before Muslims pray and recite the Qur'an, they wash in a special way called wudu. *First they wash their hands and rinse their mouth and nose. Next they wash their arms up to their elbows and then their face. They do all this three times. Then they wipe over their head and neck and finally they wash their feet. Muslims wash like this so they are clean and feel ready to start their prayer.*

Praying helps Khurram to feel calm and relaxed.

Friday prayer

On Fridays, Muslim men and boys pray with other Muslims in a mosque. This is called **Jumu'ah**. Some women and girls do this too. The person who leads the prayer is called the **Imam**. Khurram is seven years old. He likes praying with other Muslims in his community. It makes him feel that he belongs to a group that is different from his school friends and family.

Jamal is 15 years old. He lives in Yorkshire in the UK.

As I've become older, I've become more committed to Salah. When I was younger, I didn't really know why I prayed. Now, the constant reminder of God helps me live a good life as a Muslim. When I pray, God is like my closest friend. I can tell Him anything and ask for help. I can rely on Him when things get tough.

Taking on responsibility

Growing up can be an exciting time! You get to know yourself better, make new friends, explore new interests and understand more about your world. When you become a teenager, people will start to think of you as a young adult.

Choosing how to behave

Muslims believe that God knows everything they do. So, as Muslim boys and girls grow up, they learn to think carefully about how to take responsibility for their own behaviour. They may go to classes in a mosque or community centre to understand the teachings of the Qur'an better.

For example, the Qur'an says that men and women should dress and behave modestly. This means they should not show off. For women, this includes covering their hair. Some girls choose to wear a head covering called a **hijab**.

Sara has started to wear the hijab. She wants to respect the teachings of her religion.

Over to you...

● How do you think your life will be different as you become older? How will you change?

● What types of community activities are available in your area?

The Muslim way to live

Young Muslims learn how the Prophet Muhammad ﷺ taught Muslims to live. He told them to be honest, to work hard, to help their neighbours and to care for the young and old. As Muslim children grow up, they try to live like this.

Amal volunteers at a local old people's home on Sunday mornings.

When Muslims get married

Getting married is an important part of a person's life. Muslim children usually go to many weddings. It is expected that they will get married too, when they are adults.

Wedding ceremony

Most Muslims marry someone who shares the same beliefs about God. Their beliefs help them to make decisions together every day. The bride and groom must agree to marry freely. They sign a wedding contract, which mentions the gift the groom gives to the bride. The gift is called the **mahr**. It is usually a gift of money.

The Muslim wedding ceremony is called the **nikah**. A nikah can take place at a person's home, in a mosque or in a public hall. An Imam or elder Muslim conducts the ceremony.

There are many verses in the Qur'an that show that God encourages people to get married. This is one verse that is read aloud at the Muslim marriage service.

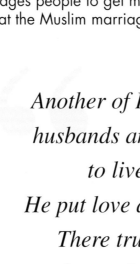

Signing the marriage contract at the Nikah.

*Another of His Signs is that He made
husbands and wives from among you
to live together in peace;
He put love and kindness between you.
There truly are Signs in that for
those who think deeply about it.*

Henna party

In some Asian, African and Arab countries, it is a popular custom to have a henna party before a wedding. The bride's hands are decorated with henna paste, made from the leaves of the henna bush. Women and girls come to the party and sing and have fun.

This bride and groom from south Asia are dressed in traditional Muslim wedding clothes.

A bride and groom exchange rings at a wedding in London.

Celebrating a new marriage

Many different customs take place around the world to celebrate a Muslim marriage. Friends and relatives help to make the celebration a very special occasion.

A meal to complete the wedding

Muslim couples invite friends, neighbours and family to share a meal with them. The meal can be fancy or simple. It is called a **walimah** and completes the Muslim wedding ceremony. It takes place on the same day as the nikah or a few days later. It's a way of letting the local community know that the couple are married.

Guests congratulate the bride and groom with an Arabic prayer the Prophet Muhammad ﷺ taught. They say this prayer to wish the couple a long and happy life together. You can read it in English on the opposite page.

These guests at a wedding party in Indonesia are eating eggs to wish the couple good luck.

"May God bless you and may blessings be upon you, and may you be happy together."

Over to you...

● What part do family and friends play in helping a Muslim couple celebrate their wedding?

● Have you been to a wedding? How did the couple show their religious beliefs?

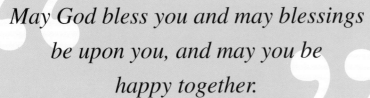

Tahmer describes his and his wife Dina's happy day.

We held our walimah in a large restaurant. Our guests included relatives who came all the way from Egypt and Germany because Dina's family is Eygyptian and my mother is German. Dina's uncle played an Egyptian wedding tune when she arrived at the walimah. Everyone had a great time!

Tahmer and Dina cut their wedding cake together.

Life together as a family

Some people send their family and friends a greetings card like this to wish them a happy Id.

Sharing is an important part of family life. Members of the family share a home, ideas and time. They celebrate special times, such as the festivals of **Ramadan** and **Id**, together.

Sharing religious beliefs

When two people get married, they decide many things together. Their faith helps them to make decisions. For example, they may both follow what it says in the Qur'an about raising children and caring for neighbours and relatives.

The Qur'an says, "Be good to your parents and relatives, and to orphans and needy, and to neighbours near and far, and the friend by your side, the traveller and to those in your care."

Salman and Laila have been married for three years.

Salman: Getting married changes your life! I learnt about the responsibility of being married from my parents and older brothers and sisters. Laila and I both work and we take care of our home together. When we plan to do anything, we make decisions together. That's not always easy!

Laila: I find married life exciting. Salman and I share lots of interests, like travelling and doing voluntary work. We do have different opinions on some things but are learning to see each other's point of view. Our faith is the most important thing we have in common as it is part of our daily life.

It is traditional for Muslims around the world to stop fasting by eating a couple of dates first.

Ramadan and Id

Ramadan is the ninth month of the Islamic calendar, in which each month starts with the new moon. During the month of Ramadan, Muslims try harder to practise their faith. They read as much of the Qu'ran as they can, and they **fast**. They do not eat or drink between dawn and dusk. Feeling hungry reminds them of people who have less than they do.

At the end of Ramadan is a day of celebration called Id. Muslim families and friends worship and celebrate together. They thank God for his blessings and stop fasting. It is a happy time of giving and sharing.

This food is for a special Id dinner to celebrate the end of Ramadan.

How it feels to grow older

Growing older can be a very special part of life, but it is often difficult too. In a Muslim community, older people are looked up to. Younger friends and family treat them with great respect and ask them for advice.

Fatima El-Amin is a retired school teacher who lives in Glasgow, Scotland.

When I was young, I was always so busy! Now that my children have grown up and have their own families I can spend more time understanding my faith. The Qur'an teaches us to give time to others in need. I like to get involved in charity work in my community. Sometimes I help to raise money for people who live where there has been a flood or other disaster. Once a week I do some voluntary work in the local hospital.

Helping the family

In a family, older relatives usually have stories to share about their life. Younger members of the family might ask them for help when they want to get married or choose a name for their baby. During celebrations, children often greet older relatives, such as their grandfather or grandmother, before anyone else.

Older people often retire, or stop working. They spend their time in different ways. They might spend time looking after their grandchildren. Some like to spend time in the community, teaching a class in the mosque or helping at a senior women's group.

This verse from the Qur'an teaches Muslims to be kind to parents, especially when they get old.

Your Lord has commanded that you should worship none but Him, and that you be kind to your parents. If either or both of them reach old age with you, say no word that shows impatience with them ...

Over to you...

- How can young people show they care for older people?

- Why do you think growing older can be hard sometimes?

- What do older people you know like to do?

Imran and his grandfather enjoy a chat. They share with each other what they have done during the day.

Some older people enjoy being a grandparent.

Young people go to older family members for advice and help.

When someone we love dies

*An Imam in Ghana, Africa, leads the funeral prayer, called the **Janazah** Prayer.*

The end of a person's life is a difficult time for family and friends. They feel sad when someone they love dies. For Muslims it is also a special time. They believe that death is just the end of a person's journey on Earth.

Life after death

Muslims believe that when someone dies, their **soul** lives on. A person's soul is the part of them that is their character and feelings. When someone hears of a person's death, they say, "To God indeed we belong and to Him indeed we shall all return." Muslims call the next life **Akhirah**, or the Hereafter. The verse from the Qu'ran on the next page describes the Hereafter.

Putting the soul to rest

All Muslims are buried when they die. The funeral is arranged as quickly as possible, to put the person's soul to rest. People come to the mosque to say prayers for the dead person. The body is washed by relatives or local people, then clothed in white cloth.

Muslims are laid to rest, or buried, facing Makkah in Saudi Arabia. It is traditional not to have large tombstones. Prophet Muhammad ﷺ recommended planting a tree where someone is buried.

> *There is a reward in this present world for those who do good, but their home in the Hereafter is far better. They will enter perpetual gardens graced with flowing streams. There they will have everything they wish.*

This Muslim graveyard in Essex is the largest in the UK.

Today some people place small headstones with the name of their relative.

People may feel lonely when someone they love dies. They miss that person. They read some verses from the Qu'ran and pray for the person.

Remembering those we loved

It is natural for relatives and friends to feel sad when someone dies. They feel upset as they remember the good times they spent together.

Always remembered

Muslims believe that when people do good work on Earth, they will be blessed in the next life when they die. They take comfort from this. They think about all the good things that a person did to help others.

Families remember the person they miss in many ways. Some people give money to a charity in their relative's name. Others give books to a school or library in memory of their relative.

A person's life is remembered by family and friends who share happy memories. They were together for special times.

Photographs help me to remember special times our family have had, such as my sister's Aqiqah, my seventh birthday and my brother's wedding.

Over to you...

● Most religions teach that there is a life after death. What do you believe happens when people die?

● How do people celebrate the lives of people who have died in your community?

My grandfather liked gardening. He liked to grow vegetables and he let me and my brother sow the seeds with him. When he got ill he carried on planting vegetables and flowers. A few months before he died, we planted a plum tree with him. Now that my grandfather isn't alive anymore, I like to go to his garden and see the plants and plum tree and remember him. I think when he died he was happy as he knew he had left things to remember him by.

Glossary and more information

Adhan The Call to Prayer.

aid Help given to people in need in poor countries.

Akhirah Life after death – the Hereafter.

Allah The name for God in *Arabic*.

Aqiqah A naming and thanksgiving celebration after a baby is born.

Arabic The language spoken in the Middle East and North Africa. The *Qur'an* was revealed in Arabic.

charity Help given out voluntarily. A charity is an organisation set up to help and protect people, animals or the environment.

fast To go without food. *Muslims* fast from dawn until dusk during *Ramadan*.

hijab A word often used to describe the head scarf or modest dress worn by *Muslim* women.

Id A religious holiday; a feast for thanking *Allah* and celebrating a happy occasion.

Imam A person who leads the prayers in a mosque.

Janazah The burial ceremony.

Jumu'ah The weekly communal *Salah* performed shortly after midday on Fridays.

mahr The wedding gift given by a groom to the bride.

Makkah The city in Saudi Arabia where the *Prophet Muhammad* ﷺ was born, and where the Sacred Mosque is.

mosque A place where *Muslims* pray.

mu'adhin One who gives the *Adhan*.

Muslim One who believes that *Allah* is the only god and that *Muhammad* is His servant and messenger.

Muhammad The name of the final *prophet*.

nikah The *Muslim* marriage ceremony.

orphan A child whose parents have died.

prophet A person who has been guided by God to teach people.

Qur'an The holy book revealed by God to the *Prophet Muhammad*.

Ramadan The ninth month of the Islamic calendar, during which *Muslims fast*.

Salah The five daily prayers to God. These are done in the way taught by the *Prophet Muhammad* and said in *Arabic*.

soul The spiritual part of a person, separate from the body.

walimah The wedding feast to celebrate a marriage in the community.

wudu A set way that *Muslims* wash before performing *Salah*.

Things to do

Invite a parent or a visitor from a mosque to talk about their wedding ceremony and celebration. Where did they get married? What happened at the wedding?

Visit a mosque by contacting one in a city, or take an e-tour of a real mosque at: www.thebcom.org/ourwork/interfaith/116-virtual-mosque-tour.html. Click on the crescent symbol to find out more about each area.

Muslims follow the example of Prophet Muhammad. Who was he? Find out about Muhammad at: atschool.eduweb.co.uk/carolrb/islam/islamintro.html

Geometric designs are popular on Id cards, in mosques and on prayer mats. Research some geometric designs to decorate a bookmark or calendar. Your card or calendar can have your own special occasions on it.

Id-ul-Adha and the Hajj are two special times of year for a Muslim. Where do Muslims go on Hajj and what do they celebrate on this Id? Find answers at www.channel4.com/culture/microsites/H/hajj

More information

Find out more about Islam on these websites or from the Muslim Education Trust.

Websites

For teachers
www.mcb.org.uk/booksforschools.php
A page on the Muslim Council of Britain website, from where you can order a resource pack designed to help primary school teachers to teach about Islam.
www.islamic-foundation.com
The online bookshop for the Islamic Foundation. As well as books, it sells "talking books", DVDs, games and posters.
www. bbc.co.uk/schools/religion/islam
A page from the BBC Schools website, giving a short introduction to Islam and some Muslim customs.

For children
www.iaw-schools.org.uk/index.php
A website offering an interactive experience on Islam. It makes it easy for pupils and teachers to find out about Islam and Muslim culture.
juniors.reonline.org.uk/
Lots of easy-to-find information about Islam and other religions. Topics include beliefs, festivals, people, history and symbols.
www.holidays.net/ramadan/muhamd.htm
Part of a website about special holidays around the world. This section contains information about the Muslim holiday of Ramadan.

Organisations

The Muslim Education Trust (MET)
130 Stroud Green Road, London, N4 3RZ
Tel: 020 7272 8502
www.muslim-ed-trust.org.uk

Index

Picture credits

The publisher would like to thank the following for their kind permission to reproduce their photographs:

Position key: c=centre; b=bottom; t=top; l=left; r=right

1: mypokcik/shutterstock; 3tr: Tahmer Mahmoud & Dina El-Sayed; 3br: Suma Din (courtesy of Vicky's Photo Magic); 4bl: Tracy Whiteside/shutterstock; 6cr: Christine Osborne/World Religions Photo Library; 7tc: Christine Osborne/World Religions Photo Library; 7cr: Juan Monino/iStockphoto; 7br: iStockphoto; 8cl: Zahid Jawed; 8bl: Tracy Whiteside/shutterstock; 9c:

Claire Stout/World Religions Photo Library; 10bl: Arslan Nusrat (courtesy of Muslim Hands); 10br: Arslan Nusrat (Muslim Hands); 11c: Arslan Nusrat (Muslim Hands); 12bl: Christine Osborne/World Religions Photo Library; 13c Distinctive Images/shutterstock; 14cl: Christine Osborne/World Religions Photo Library; 14bc: Christine Osborne/World Religions Photo Library; 15t: Tim Gurney/World Religions Photo Library; 15c: Glenda M Powers/shutterstock; 16l: Claire Stout/World Religions Photo Library; 17c: Ramzi Hachicho/shutterstock; 18cl: Salman & Laila Siddiqui; 18bl: Salman & Laila Siddiqui; 19tl: Claire Stout/World Religions Photo Library; 19c: Paul Gapper/World Religions Photo Library; 20b: Christine Osborne/World Religions Photo Library; 21c: Tahmer Mahmoud & Dina El-Sayed; 21bl: Tahmer

Mahmoud & Dina El-Sayed; 22cl: Christine Osborne/ World Religions Photo Library; 22bl: Salman & Laila Siddiqui; 23t: Louise B Duran/World Religions Photo Library; 23br: Christine Osborne/World Religions Photo Library; 24cl: Ramzi Hachicho/shutterstock; 25c: Jabbar Khan & Yusuf Khan (courtesy of Kishor Raghoobar Jr); 26cl: Christine Osborne/World Religions Photo Library; 27c: Christine Osborne/World Religions Photo Library; 28tr: Claire Stout/World Religions Photo Library; 28cr: mypokcik/shutterstock; 28br: Tahmer Mahmoud & Dina El-Sayed; 29c: Suma Din (courtesy of Vicky's Photo Magic); 29l: Chas/shutterstock

Cover photograph © Jon Arnold Images Ltd/Alamy